Training for Discipleship

by Robert G. Middleton

Manual for Church Membership Preparation

JUDSON PRESS • VALLEY FORGE

TRAINING FOR DISCIPLESHIP

Library of Congress Cataloging in Publication Data

Middleton, Robert G.
  Training for discipleship.

  Includes bibliographical references.
  1. Church membership—Handbooks, manuals, etc.
I. Title.
BV820.M48   286'.131   75-33239
ISBN 0-8170-0659-1

Printed in the U.S.A. ⊕

CONTENTS

Introduction

This manual seeks to answer three questions:
1. Why should churches be concerned about training for membership?
2. How can churches go about the task of training for church membership?
3. What should be the content of such training?

With these three questions in mind, the manual is intended as a guide for those persons within Baptist churches who are concerned about doing a more effective job in training for authentic discipleship. Training in discipleship is essential for the deeper growth of persons in Christian faith and the increased effectiveness of the churches.

Certain assumptions have guided the preparation and writing. These assumptions have grown out of the awareness of the varied life of our American Baptist churches. A basic assumption is this: there is no *one* way in which to do the task of membership training. Another assumption is that the variety of our churches must be kept in mind at all times. These churches, spread across the land, are of all kinds. Small and large; rural, suburban, and urban; flourishing and struggling; fundamentalist, liberal, and conservative; old and new— these are only a few of the different characteristics of our churches. It is this variety which makes it impossible to devise one way which will fit all situations.

A final, basic assumption does not deal with the specifics but with a conviction about the importance of this matter in our churches. The task facing the current Christian generation is staggering in its demands. It can be met only if we give attention to careful training. "Church life as usual" is simply not good enough. Our aim is clear: to help persons to live responsibly under the lordship of Jesus Christ in the fellowship of his people for witness and service in the world.

CHAPTER 1

The Need
for a
New Strategy

A great many things have changed in the course of the history of the Christian church. One element, however, has remained constant. It has always been the responsibility of the church to make disciples. The church can be faithful to its Lord only if it takes seriously the task of bringing persons to authentic discipleship.

It is important to get this clear at the outset. Of course, there are additional responsibilities the church must seek to fulfill, but authentic discipleship is the foundation upon which everything rests. Without willingness to accept what Bonhoeffer called "the cost of discipleship," there can be no real effectiveness on the part of the church.

DISCIPLESHIP DYNAMICS

The sweep of discipleship is caught up in three strong verbs—**come, abide,** and **go.**

Discipleship begins when the person hears the call of Jesus, "Come to me . . ." (Matthew 11:28). Nothing else can be the starting point of Christian living. Persons may well respond to such a call in a variety of ways. For some the call will be an emotional experience that is like being born again or being brought into life out of death. For others the call may come in the midst of ordinary tasks and in a calm manner. There can be no stereotyping of the response, suggesting that only a particular way can be accepted as valid. When Christ's "Come to me" is answered by the response of the person, the Christian life commences.

That response to Christ, though essential, is not sufficient to sustain the ongoing venture of discipleship. Accordingly, Jesus added to the call an exhortation in which he urged that his followers "Abide in me, and I in you. As the branch cannot bear fruit by itself, unless it abides in the vine, neither can you, unless you abide in me" (John

7

15:4). It is never possible for anyone to learn all there is to know of Jesus, nor is it possible to arrive at some point beyond which further growth is impossible or unnecessary. There is another dimension of this living in Christ which needs to be stressed. We are simply unable to fulfill the calling of Christ apart from the experience of living deeply in him. For that kind of task, we need to know Christ as pardon and as power, a mercy that forgives and a strength that empowers.

There is another aspect of Christian existence which follows the response and the abiding. Jesus calls us to live under his lordship and to abide in him in order that we can be sent to witness to him and for him in the world he loves. Always this imperative must be faced. The purpose of the church, as H. Richard Niebuhr put it, is to increase the love of God and neighbor. Another way of stating the purpose of the church is the Great Commission given by Jesus: "Go therefore and make disciples of all nations, baptizing them in the name of the Father and of the Son and of the Holy Spirit" (Matthew 28:19).

If you look at the functioning of the church in the light of these three emphases of Jesus—come, abide, go—you will note that we have been reasonably faithful in setting forth the call to discipleship. Once that call has been issued and a response made, we have stressed with some consistency the call to go into all the world. Preparation for church membership is not by any means the only kind of training needed; it is simply one aspect of the training which needs to be done. But it is one of the areas where we have failed to measure up to our responsibility.

BARRIERS TO DISCIPLESHIP

What explains our failure to take the matter of training in discipleship with real seriousness? Look at a few reasons which may explain, even if they do not justify, our neglect at this point.

For one thing, we have depended upon emotion as though it were capable of carrying the entire load of Christian discipleship. Rightly emphasizing the fact that commitment to Jesus Christ involves the emotions, we have failed to see that such emotional power remains undirected and diffused unless something is added to it. Note the way this is put, because it is important to get the point clear. Emotional emphasis is not wrong; it is only incomplete. No vital Christian faith can ever be separated from a vibrant emotional quality. But to rest the matter at that point is to confuse the starting point with the destination.

It is now becoming clear that we cannot afford to trust in feeling alone. It has left a legacy of anti-intellectualism in our religious life. Since we have not taken the time to ground persons in the truth, giving them good solid reasons for believing, we have seen many lose their faith when they have come up against alternative explanations or when they have undergone disturbing experiences. Their fervent emotion has not been sufficient to see them through such times of testing.

Once again, we have failed to take preparation for discipleship seriously because we have not considered it essential. We were complacent because we had always had allies upon whom we could count to do the work of training. Once the church had brought the person to the point of commitment to Christ, these other agencies could be counted upon to bring the matter to completion.

The home, for example, was once a strong ally of the church in the task of Christian training and nurture. Much could be left to this agency. Whatever you may now think of the home, there are few who would deny that the home is no longer able to function with great effectiveness in the training of people in Christian faith. Without exaggeration it can be said that the home, once the church's helper, now needs help itself.

For a long time the public school was something of an ally. The values of the public school were generally those of Protestant Christianity, and the school building in many communities was almost an adjunct of the church. What was propagated was not, of course, an explicit and denominational Christianity, but the school nevertheless provided an atmosphere in which the task of the church was made easier because both shared in a commitment to certain truths. It is clear now that this sort of cooperation is a thing of the past. The church can no longer count upon the school to do its job for it or even to share in it at all.

This brings us to one other ally which should be mentioned. Like the public schools, American culture was for a long time self-consciously Christian. I do not want to get involved in the argument about whether the culture was really Christian or not; that is unnecessary in light of our purpose here. It is at least clear that Americans were sure that the nation and the culture were Christian. This kind of self-awareness prepared the way, if it did not actually do the job, of bringing persons into Christian faith. There is little point in trying to determine whether our contemporary culture has authentic Christian elements in it. It is enough to note that more and more observers are agreed in describing the culture in terms such as "secular" or "post-Christian" or "pagan."

In addition to dependence upon emotion and confidence in allies, we have failed to take training seriously because we have come close to losing what is distinctive about the Christian life. More and more we have slipped into the snare of moralism. We have persuaded ourselves that being a Christian is simply another way of saying that we are "good people." We have defined the Christian life as though the essence of the matter were in the avoidance of certain "sins" and the cultivation of inoffensive virtues. It became very easy, as a result, to persuade ourselves that nothing very rigorous was to be expected of people and hence no training was required.

Along with moralism has gone an ethical idealism. This finds expression in the conviction that the Christian life is a matter of being active in good causes.

Those who stress moralism and ethical idealism have clearly put emphasis upon important and essential matters of Christian living. Christianity *is* a way of life, and it does involve a commitment to worthy causes. These things are part—and a very important part—of what it means to be a Christian. A discipleship which does not issue in worthy daily living is counterfeit. But there is much more to the Christian experience than this.

Honesty compels us to add one final admission to this list of reasons for our failure. We must confess our apathy. To do an adequate job of training in discipleship is not easy. It requires a considerable amount of time and training. We have not been willing to give that kind of commitment to the task.

The upshot of all this is that churches vary greatly in their approach to this matter of training for authentic discipleship. The variety can be illustrated by describing the practices of three churches.

VARIETIES OF RESPONSE

Church #1 has no training at all. A person who makes a decision for Jesus Christ is baptized immediately. After that event has taken place, sometimes on the very day of the decision, there may be an attempt to persuade the person to enroll in Bible study or in other groups in the church. But such enrollment is not required and sometimes nothing more is done.

Church #2 proceeds on a somewhat different basis. In this church, also, the decision is important. Once that decision is made, there is a period of instruction in the rudiments of Christian faith and in the particular emphases of that congregation. The length of such instruction varies, depending upon the background of the person. Usually, however, such instruction precedes baptism or is a requirement following baptism. The church manifests a degree of seriousness about the matter, but it has never really looked at the process carefully. There is no long-range strategy involved, and no clear goals have been established.

Church #3, as a result of a period of study and reflection, became dissatisfied with its way of preparation for discipleship. The study, which was carried on over a period of time, eventually led to the adoption of a comprehensive program of preparation. The entire educational program of the church was examined; questions were asked about where there were emphases which were designed to make both discipleship and church membership meaningful experiences. Where there were gaps, the church moved to meet such gaps with programs and materials of its own devising. When the study was completed, it was examined by the boards and finally adopted by the church as its settled policy. The program, which was viewed as a process extending during the entire Christian life of the person, included training of many kinds. The regular curriculum of the church school was utilized. In addition, special study groups were set up to deal with a variety of emphases. Special classes were used for young people prior to baptism and for adults joining the church from other communions. This kind of approach will be presented in more detail in later pages, but it is described in this brief fashion here in order to indicate something of the thrust intended by this manual.

TOWARD REAL DISCIPLESHIP

What, then, makes the difference in these churches? It rests, I suggest, on a deepened awareness in two areas.

The first area is that of a realistic recognition of the nature of the world in which the modern Christian must live and witness. Whatever else may be said about it, it is a dramatically changed world. We have all been made aware of "future shock" and have been forced to recognize that change has speeded up fantastically in our day. This means that the Christian must live in a world where many of the old certainties have been brought into question and where standards, once accepted without skepticism, are now under critical scrutiny everywhere.

It will do no good for the church to try to hide from this kind of world. Nostalgia will not enable us to escape; it will only make us ineffective. Pious protestations that everything is really all right will prevent us from being ready to deal with the world as it is actually experienced by Christian people.

Focus your attention for a moment on the person who has made the commitment to Jesus Christ. Follow that person out into the world of everyday and what does the person come up against?

Morally the person confronts the challenge of living in a time when the standards are shifting. Absolutes to guide conduct have disappeared, and the Christian lives in the midst of a society where hosts of people believe that right and wrong are meaningless terms. The self becomes the arbiter of morality. Illustrations of this can be provided by all of us in our daily experience.

Intellectually the person is sent into a world where there are currents of opinion running which challenge everything he or she believes. The Christian will live in a culture which has been powerfully shaped by the impact of science and technology. These triumphs produce in people either a veneration of science as a new messiah or a paralyzing apprehension about its power. A number of alternative views of human life and destiny assail the mind. The person sent to live in such a world as a Christian but without the very best kind of training which can possibly be provided is vulnerable and defenseless.

Spiritually the Christian is sent to live in a world which is very religious. It is religious in the same sense in which Paul described the citizens of Athens as being "very religious" (see Acts 17:22ff.). It is crucial to see that the spiritual problem of our day is not doubt; it is idolatry. Doubt is perhaps an easier obstacle to overcome than is idolatry. Yet a moment's reflection will surely make clear the fact that ours is a "very religious" age. People believe in a host of things—in communism, in scientism, in secularism, in occultism, in astrology. The list is almost endless. What is clear is that the Christian has no way whatever by which to be kept immune from the challenge of competing faiths. If the Christian is to maintain commitment to Jesus Christ in the face of such competing claims, there is urgent need to train such a person in the Christian faith so that he or she can give an intelligent defense of what is believed.

If you let your focus rest upon the Christian person, living day by day in such a world, you can see the need for careful training. This is no less true if you let your focus rest upon the church itself, for the church must bear its witness through its members in precisely this kind of world.

The second area which leads a church to take seriously training for discipleship is a recognition of what love and concern for the person really mean. Such training is a response on the part of the church to the claims of love.

The church, at least in its ideal form, is a supportive fellowship. In that fellowship persons bear one another's burdens and share their joys. The dimension of love was so real that it marked the Christian community in the New Testament period as something new and distinctive. "How these Christians love one another!" was the cry of an impressed world.

Our trouble today is that we can see that love requires us to bear burdens and to share joys and sorrows, but we do not see the fullest and most effective training of persons as being, in its way, a manifestation of love and caring. The idea has persisted that the Christian church has little responsibility for training the minds of its people. Yet we are urged to be able to give a reason for the faith that is in us. Effective witnessing is a matter of knowing what one believes with sufficient clarity to be able to defend it against those who would attack it and to commend it to those who seek to understand it.

In summary, then, it does not matter whether you look at the lives of persons living as Christians in the modern world or at the church as the fellowship of such believers called to witness to Jesus Christ. In either case, there is no way by which Christians in their personal witnessing or the church in its corporate mission can be effective without careful training.

Let's assume for a moment that we are agreed about the need for training. A question comes before us: How can a church prepare itself to assume this important responsibility? That question will form the basis for our next chapter.

CHAPTER 2

Outline
of a
Strategy

There are three essential steps to be taken by any church which seeks to be effective in training persons for authentic discipleship:

Step #1: Analysis and evaluation of present practice

Step #2: Determination of goals and objectives

Step #3: Choice of means by which to arrive at objectives.

This chapter seeks to sketch a way by which the first two steps may be taken. The following chapters will suggest possible means of implementing Step #3.

CONCERN: THE STARTING POINT

Any significant change in the matter of training and preparation will take place only if someone gets concerned about the situation. The easy thing is simply to go along doing what has been done and trusting that it will somehow prove sufficient. Change must be engendered in the face of this tendency to let things go as they are.

Where will this impetus toward change come from? There seems to be no way of accomplishing change in this area in most of our churches without the real concern of the pastor. If the pastor does not persistently press for a better way, the church is not likely to be concerned about the matter.

Accordingly, the pastor needs to take a careful look at the case outlined in the first chapter. If the pastor believes that the argument is essentially sound and that we need to do something to improve our procedures, the way is prepared for the church to take a similar look.

On a more hopeful note, let's suppose that the pastor has taken a look at the current Christian scene. Let us suppose, furthermore, that this view has left the pastor with a conviction that new approaches are called for: Where do we go from that point?

STEP #1

The church is then on the threshold of Step #1, which is the analysis and evaluation of present practice. This is the place where the venture must involve the congregation and not the pastor only.

The concern needs to rise out of the daily life and experience of the congregation. In any given setting, the approach of the pastor must be suggested by the situation of the particular church. Consider, however, a couple of examples of ways by which it might be done.

We are all familiar by now with the fact that the membership of most churches can be pictured in terms of three concentric circles. The inner circle is composed of those who are active and committed. Around this inner core is the circle of those who are somewhat involved. The outside circle is composed of those who are inactive. Every church I know has some of each of these types.

Suppose that the pastor were to focus attention on that group of inactive persons. Perhaps the board of deacons, facing up to the task of keeping the membership records accurate, would be the place to do this. At any rate, the names of persons in that category are reviewed by the board. At that point, the pastor can raise the essential questions: What happened to these persons? Why did they become inactive? At some moment in their lives, all of these persons in baptism promised to follow Jesus Christ. What caused them to forsake that commitment?

Obviously, it would be an oversimplification to say that the cause was *no real training* or *inadequate training*. But such a way of approaching the matter would lead the board to take a careful look at what is currently being done by the church.

Another way of helping a congregation to face its responsibility might be to establish a study group, made up in part at least of church officers, on some such theme as "Christians in an Unchristian Society." The focus would be on the society as it actually functions. How does the believer live and witness in such a society? From that point, it should be made clear that such a setting for Christian witness demands careful preparation.

One other suggestion is offered. Every congregation needs to discover periodically where its people are in terms of their understanding of Christian faith and its meaning for human existence. A religious belief inventory might be shared with the congregation. What are the *real* understandings people have of God, the meaning of Jesus Christ, the nature of the church, the significance of the cross, and other areas of Christian belief? Just as important would be the discovery of how these beliefs relate to the daily existence of Christians in society. Such a study would show that there is widespread confusion in regard to beliefs and much actual error. Out of such a study might well come a willingness to look at procedures with a careful scrutiny.

Assuming for a moment that the analysis and evaluation have taken place, what is the next step? Step #2 is the determination of goals and objectives. This is a crucial step. It is crucial because without a clear idea of what is being sought, the means determined upon will be vague and ineffective.

GOALS AND OBJECTIVES

Recall now the three words suggested in chapter 1: **come, abide,** and **go.** In elaboration of the implications of these words, it is clear that discipleship preparation includes at least three vital elements.

Come

The first element is the decision of the person in regard to the claim of Jesus Christ. This claim is at the heart of the Christian faith. Without some clear decision about Christ, there can be no start in the Christian life.

The response of the person should not be forced into a type. It is essential to recognize that God deals with us on a very personal basis, and no single way can be made normative for all.

The person should not be manipulated in such fashion that the decision when made is forced or artificial. This is a proper caution to be observed in dealing with any age, but it should be especially stressed in dealing with the years of adolescence. During that time, peer pressure is very strong, and the temptation is real to use such pressure to force a decision for Christ. It is often said, "If we don't get the young persons then, we'll never get them." Even when this is not said in so many words, it is the implicit assumption upon which the training session operates. It is, however, unworthy and betrays a lack of trust in the Spirit. The task is to present the claim of Christ and to trust in the Spirit to elicit the response. Ours is not the responsibility for the response, since we never bring redemption to anyone. This is God's work in the soul. It was the Quaker George Fox who said the right thing in this regard: "I took men to Jesus Christ and left them there." This is the real task of discipleship training. It is faithless on our part to do less than present Christ; it is presumptuous for us to attempt to do more.

Abide

The second element in discipleship training is the incorporation of the person into the community of faith. This incorporation is essential, because there is no such thing as individualistic Christianity. This point needs to be stressed. The notion has been widely accepted that the church is somehow to be regarded as a kind of superfluous appendage of Christian faith.

The New Testament, however, knows nothing of this type of private Christianity. It is a book which treats faith as a communal reality. Individualistic Christianity is a contradiction in terms. From the point of view of the New Testament, you cannot be "in Christ," to use one of the great terms, without being in his body—and that means the church.

The specific nature of this incorporation will be set forth in later pages. Here we need to note only that this involves helping the Christian to sense involvement in the biblical community, which means appropriating the decisive events of Old and New Testaments and seeing the bearing of those events upon the formation of faith and witness today, and membership in the historic community of the church universal, the company of those who affirm the lordship of Jesus Christ. The Christian must also become involved in the life and work of our own denomination as the place where the chance is afforded to serve Jesus Christ and to find a supportive fellowship and day by day to share in the life of a particular local church, the place where the reality of the Christian community takes shape and form for the believer.

Go

The third element in this matter of discipleship training is the preparation of the Christian believer to share in God's mission in the world. Emphasis has been placed in these pages upon the necessity of bringing the person into a relation to Jesus Christ that is expressed in responsible sharing in the life and work of the church. That stress has, I believe, a continuing validity, and we need not be hesitant or apologetic about it. But neither can we rest content when the person has been brought to affirm Christ's lordship and to accept participation in the church's life as part of that discipleship. We believe that God has a mission in the world for the sake of persons, and Christian believers are those persons who seek to join God in his mission. It is impossible to confine God's mission to the church alone; therefore the Christian is involved in mission to the world in the world.

PLANNING THE NEXT STEP

What has happened to this point? If the first two steps have been followed, the congregation has taken a hard look at its present practice. It has determined either that it is fully satisfied with what is being done or that there are areas that need to be given new attention. Out of this has come a consideration of the threefold nature of discipleship preparation: the relation to Christ (come), the incorporation into the church (abide), and the joining with God in his mission in the world (go).

The danger, however, is that such a process of discussion and study may remain an academic exercise. In order to prevent this, the congregation as a whole needs to consider the report on present practice and the statement of goals and objectives.

In whatever way is appropriate in a given congregation, the development of specific plans and programs needs to be delegated to a responsible group. It may be the board of deacons or the board of Christian education or a special task force created for this purpose alone. In addition, given our tendency to put things off, there should be some kind of time schedule worked out.

In all honesty, it must be acknowledged that there is a sticky question hovering at the edges of our entire discussion. It is the vexing question of discipline in the modern church. Accordingly, churches need to face with new candor the question of what is properly to be expected of those who commit themselves to Jesus Christ. Two errors need to be avoided.

On one side is the error of being indifferent. In altogether too many instances, to become a member of the church is an action which can be taken with no thought whatever that it might involve the person in accepting any real responsibilities.

In this situation, we need to ponder seriously the contention of Geddes MacGregor:

> The result of the inevitable revolt against such practices has been that the spirit of discipline has so far declined as to make the very word sound archaic to modern Protestant ears. Yet whatever the mistakes of our

fathers in applying it, Christian discipline remains absolutely indispensable for the life of the Church. . . . Discipline is the yoke of Christ.[1]

The error opposite to that of being indifferent is that of legalism. Our revulsion against this error is right; legalism is an affront to the meaning of the Christian gospel. It is the attempt to make conformity to outward rules and regulations substitute for the commitment to follow Jesus Christ. What invariably happens is that such legalism produces a couple of unfortunate results.

One is a spirit of harsh and often loveless judgments. Persons are rejected in terms of their fidelity or lack of it to these rules. Since rules are fairly objective standards, it is easy to single out the person who fails. By condemning such, the rest of the people feed the fires of their own self-righteousness. In the end, legalism proves harsh to those who are condemned and spiritually perilous to those who do the condemning.

The other result of legalism is that it invariably results in standards for the Christian life which are fairly easy to observe. Having been made by persons, they are not beyond attainment. They will almost always be found in the category of outward behavior, usually in terms of institutional loyalty, and rarely deal with the matter of relations to other human beings. Any system which produces at one and the same time a system inducing self-righteousness and a too easy type of Christian existence is a bad system.

The question that needs to be confronted is: what does authentic discipleship call for? The determination of what is involved should be carefully considered by the body of believers. When that consideration has been given, there needs to be a corporate decision whose intention will be to provide a context within which persons can express their commitment to Jesus Christ.

The program outlined in this chapter is admittedly ambitious and somewhat threatening. It will take time and effort, and it may induce discomfort in the fellowship. There is no point in denying such possibilities. Without such a program, however, we are reduced to the continuation of present practices and to the current level of Christian effectiveness. And in this kind of world, who will really believe such responses adequate?

[1]Geddes MacGregor, *The Coming Reformation* (Philadelphia: The Westminster Press, 1960), p. 65.

CHAPTER 3

Children
in the
Church

Thus far we have been engaged in two enterprises. One was to develop *concern* about discipleship training. A second was to suggest a *context* within which such training can be effectively carried on. It has been essential to do these things, because without concern no attempt will be made to improve present practices or to introduce new ones. And without a context of theological soundness no techniques are likely to be effective.

Now, however, it is time to come to grips with the matter of *content*. In this connection, I want to share in this and the following chapters a considerable amount of material—outlines, letters, and materials. These are only suggestions and are not meant to be followed slavishly. Indeed, the real value of this material will be in its capacity to stimulate you to devise your own materials. Since it is often easier to do that when you have something against which to react, these materials are shared here. By all means, use what is of value in your situation; but do some dreaming and experimenting on your own. My fundamental conviction is that we can stand a great deal of trial-and-error; what we cannot stand is an apathetic maintenance of present indifference.

A PROCESS, NOT AN EVENT

If we are to improve our work in the development of authentic discipleship, we must change some of our ways of approaching the task. It is not sufficient to see discipleship preparation as an event occurring in the years of adolescence, quite unrelated to what has gone before. A comprehensive view is one which sees this as a process in which church and home are involved from the time of a child's birth to the point of decision for discipleship—and beyond that point, since the task of Christian growth never really ends.

There has always been confusion about the place of the child in the

21

church. The problem exists not only for those churches which practice infant baptism but for Baptist churches as well. This issue has not been satisfactorily resolved.

The problems faced by churches which practice infant baptism can be left to them to face, but we need to give some thought to the place of the child in our Baptist churches. The child is not a member of the church; that is something which must await his or her baptism. But this surely cannot mean that the child is totally outside the church. Nor can it mean that the child is a child of wrath and not of promise. The grace of Christ is present in the child, just as it is present in the world. Christ loved and gave himself for the world, and that world is the object of his redemptive love. At the same time, however, the truth of the grace of Christ has not been accepted by the child until it is made real through the total life of the Christian community. The child's act of decision does not create the truth; it simply makes it truth for the child. Then the child is ready for baptism.

Walter Harrelson has put this matter well:

> Children in the church belong to Christ at birth, precisely because they belong to the human race which in Jesus Christ has been redeemed from its bondage to sin, death and decay. Children outside the church also belong to Christ at birth, regardless of whether their parents are Christians. But children in the church are being shaped to discern the truth of their lives. They live in connection with those who affirm this truth and who seek to display it in the totality of their existence in the world—the new world which Christ has redeemed.[1]

The church, as a community of love and concern, seeks to make it possible for children to come to this awareness.

NEED FOR VISIBLE SIGNS

This responsibility is likely to be vital in the church only if ways are found by which the congregation can be kept aware. Some visible actions are necessary, which will keep the people of the church conscious of responsibility for the Christian nurture of children.

A few years ago the church I now serve became concerned about the place of children in its fellowship. A committee of lay persons was appointed to study the matter and to report to the congregation, suggesting an overall program and determining ways by which to bring the whole church to an awareness of what was being done.

Certain basic assumptions guided the committee in its work.

---

[1]Walter J. Harrelson, "Children in the Church," *Foundations,* vol. 6, no. 2 (April, 1963), p. 142.

Nurture is necessary long before the experience of definite commitment in believer's baptism. This nurture must involve the individual as a total person; it must include the intellect (thinking), the emotions (feeling), and the physical body (doing and behavior). All three must be included if the process is to be complete.

The basic purpose is that all persons be made aware of God through his self-disclosure, especially his redeeming love in Jesus Christ. Out of such awareness would come persons who will—

1. know who they are and what their human situation means;
2. grow as sons and daughters of God, rooted in the Christian community;
3. live in obedience to the will of God in every relationship;
4. fulfill their common vocation in the world; and
5. abide in Christian hope.[2]

At certain points in the life of the child, the involvement of the church in the child's life needs to be made visible. One of the first such times is in the context of the service of parental dedication. It is important that this service be approached in a serious manner. It is not something perfunctory and ceremonial.

The vital matter of cooperation between home and church needs to be established at this point. It is very important that the pastor call in the home of parents and at that time go over very carefully the promises they are to make in the service of worship. It should be stressed at such a time that there is a serious element of hypocrisy in making affirmations in the service of worship with no real intention of fulfilling them afterward. Some churches, disturbed at being in the position of aiding in such hypocrisy, refuse to permit parents who are not themselves professing Christians and members of the church to participate in such services. Other churches insist that one of the parents be a professing Christian. No matter what regulations govern the matter, the pastor has the responsibility of helping the parents to face honestly the commitments they will make. Only if they understand the nature of the commitments and seriously intend to act upon them, should the service take place.

If the home has a responsibility, the congregation is no less involved. It is a merit of the service provided in John Skoglund's *A Manual of Worship* that the place of the congregation is recognized. In the service, the minister says: "Do you, as members of this congregation, acknowledge and accept the responsibility, together

---

[2]See *Foundations for Curriculum* (Valley Forge: American Baptist Board of Education and Publication, 1966), p. 13.

with the parents, of teaching and training this child, that he (she), being brought up in the discipline and instruction of the Lord, may be led in due time to trust Christ as Savior, and confessing him as Lord in baptism, be made a member of his Church? If so, will you signify your acceptance of this responsibility by standing?"[3] It is, of course, no more than a symbolic gesture; but it is a step toward the creation of awareness.

One other modest symbolic gesture is followed. In the mimeographed or printed booklet containing the roster of the church constituency, the names of children in church families are included. An appropriate marking indicates that they are not full members of the church, but their presence is another way of saying that they are in a real sense part of the Christian fellowship.

A second time in which the church expresses in visible fashion its responsibility for the Christian nurture of children occurs when the child is in the third grade. At that time, once again in the service of worship so that the entire church is aware of it, a Bible is presented. Time is taken to say why the church is doing this. The act itself speaks of the importance the church places upon knowledge of the Bible. Parents are notified by letter of this action, and their presence is encouraged. In the actual presentation, care is taken to suggest ways by which the family can be involved in making the Bible a living book in the lives of all.

The next year, when the child reaches the fourth grade, the preparation is intensified. A special course of instruction is given to the children, including two major units of study—one on the Bible and the other on Christian holidays and celebrations. Each unit contains three sessions which are taught in the church school period or in an expanded session. The teaching is done either by a minister or by specially trained lay persons. In conformity with the conviction that the church as a whole must be informed, full information about the venture is shared with the church. What is being done is known by all persons.

Since the cooperation of the home is essential, care is taken to share with parents full information concerning what will be done. The course of study to be followed is made known, and the cooperation of the home is enlisted. In the actual working out of the sessions, every opportunity is taken to include studies or activities which of necessity involve the parents.

[3]John E. Skoglund, *A Manual of Worship* (Valley Forge: Judson Press, 1968), pp. 236-237.

At the fifth grade level, another special course is offered. There are three sessions about the church, drawing upon material about the early church in the Bible and explorations of the church today. A second unit of four sessions is focused on worship, including planning and participation in the worship of the congregation.

Discipleship training thus includes, in addition to the emphases which are part of the church school curriculum, special emphases during each of three years—third, fourth, and fifth grades. No claim is made that such careful preparation alone will do the job, but there is surely no justification for doing less than we are capable of doing.

Other churches may want to develop their own methods of emphasizing the involvement of children in the life of the church. Whatever specific steps are taken, these visible indications of the importance of training for discipleship will help boys and girls of the church to be ready for the sessions which will focus directly upon their commitment to Jesus Christ, participation in believer's baptism, and full membership in the church.

CHAPTER 4

The World
of
Adolescence

A well-known passage in Ecclesiastes tells us that "For everything there is a season, and a time for every matter under heaven" (Ecclesiastes 3:1). If there is indeed a time for all the matters cited in the passage, there is also a time in a person's life when the challenge of Christian commitment can be effectively presented. Of course, it is not a case of then or never; but long experience has shown that during the years of adolescence there is an openness to the claim of commitment which is greater than at other periods of life.

Even without the benefit of psychological expertise, religious groups understood this basic fact. Adolescence is the time of rites of passage. The early years of adolescence are the period when the Jewish young person experiences Bar Mitzvah. In churches which have practiced infant baptism, the rite of confirmation is administered in the years of early adolescence. Clearly, human experience suggested the appropriateness of a practice, even if there was no psychological theory to justify it.

This background provides us with reasonable confidence that we are on the right track when we give special attention to the years of early adolescence. It is within those years that most discipleship training will take place.

There are several purposes we need to keep in mind in this chapter. We want to indicate the principles which are to guide us in discipleship training. Then we want to be sure we understand the various types of young people who will be part of such training. If we are to work with real effectiveness, we shall have to understand some of the qualities of adolescence.

PRINCIPLES

One note has sounded through the pages of this manual, perhaps to the point of weariness. It has been a stress on the importance of training for Christian discipleship. The point needs to be stated again as we come to the specifics of how the job is to be done.

What is required is that the congregation and the young persons share a sense of how important this matter really is. There are some actions which will help to make real that importance. The full participation of the minister is essential. This is not to say that he or she must be the teacher of the sessions for the young people. It is to say that the pastor must be involved in the selection and training of the persons who are going to do the actual teaching. As a general policy, this area should be seen as a ministerial responsibility, and exceptions should be permitted only in the light of important considerations.

A second procedure that will emphasize the importance of the training is to put the sessions at a special time. Attendance at all sessions should be insisted upon. If a session is missed, there should be an expectation that it will be made up.

Along this same line, the sessions should be so planned that definite assignments are made. Young people will take seriously and respect only what the congregation itself takes seriously and also treats with respect.

A final suggestion is to have the sessions move toward a goal—the decision of the young person in regard to the claim of Jesus Christ. No one can judge another's response to that claim; that is a matter of the relation of the person to Christ. Nevertheless, there should be an interview between the young person and the board of deacons or a committee of the board. (The pastor may also need to prepare the deacons for this task.) It should not be an inquisition, but a genuine attempt to understand what the young persons have come to know about the Christian faith through the sessions. The purpose of the interview is not to express a judgment but to make real a concern.

The pivotal importance of discipleship training is our first principle.

A second principle is the avoidance of pressure or manipulation. In the years of adolescence, peer group pressure is extremely strong. If several young persons are committed to baptism and church membership, they will often put pressure upon another young person. Such pressure is very hard to resist. Sometimes leaders of sessions are not careful to refrain from unwarranted manipulation. It is often implied, even if it is not actually said, that young persons must be won during these sessions or they may never be won at all. Imbued with that outlook, the leaders may utilize pressures and emotional appeals that overwhelm the young person. A decision is made, but it is often made in response to external pressures rather than as an assent of the inner being.

Christian dealing with human beings must be based upon the integrity of personhood. It is wrong to violate that personhood, even if the motives seem noble indeed. The person has the right to say yes or no, and that answer must be respected.

A third principle is closely aligned with the second. The integrity of the person is to be respected. So must the integrity of the gospel be respected. It must be remembered that the *fundamental* purpose of discipleship training is not to make church members but to develop disciples of Jesus Christ. Such a goal is not achievable except on the basis of the integrity of the gospel. There should be no toning down of the demands of Christ in the hope that in such form they will meet with more response. What then happens is that the person responds to some substitute for the gospel, and the venture of Christian discipleship loses its glow and glory. There is, after all, a certain blunt demand: "If any man would come after me, let him deny himself and take up his cross and follow me" (Matthew 16:24). Jesus never attempted to enlist followers on any basis other than that of reality. We often are involved in toning down the demands, sometimes consciously, most of the time unconsciously. We probably do so because we are still victims of the success demon, and we find it hard to believe that it is more important to be faithful than to be "sucessful" in worldly terms.

These, then, are the principles we need to guide us: a sense of importance, an avoidance of manipulation or pressure, and a firm commitment to the integrity of the gospel.

TYPES OF YOUNG PEOPLE

Almost every congregation will have within it young people who come from widely varying religious backgrounds. Such backgrounds need to be understood by those who are planning and conducting the discipleship training. This obviously requires a depth of real acquaintance with the young persons. Each must be seen in his or her uniqueness and approached with that background in mind. In short, they are not just "young people," a vague and undifferentiated mass. They are individual and unique persons, each with a name, a family situation, a background, and needs peculiar to the person.

Some of the young persons will be from families which have had a long and active relationship to the church. The young persons have always been involved, and the parents have taken their church relationship seriously. The church has found in such homes real partners in the task of Christian nurture.

Other young persons will come from families which are on the periphery of the church. There is some activity connected with the church, but it is sporadic and uncertain. The home in such cases is not really a partner and sometimes, because of its lack of real commitment, is an obstacle. It is important to see that such homes and family groups need to be kept informed of what is being done. Ways can often be devised to involve the parents in the process at some points. If this is done with skill, it is often possible to establish new and firmer ties to the church on the part of the families involved. Sometimes the young persons can be asked to interview their parents about the role of religion in their lives. Or they can make a survey to discover what their parents seek in the church. By all means, the material to be covered by the young persons should be communicated to the parents. A pastoral call can serve useful purposes here; it can make sure the material is shared, and it can help the parents to face seriously their own church relationship.

The procedure in both instances cited is clear. There will be some young persons, however, who have been attracted to the church but whose home has no connection and little if any interest. Our mandate to share the Good News and to witness to our faith surely applies in this regard. The indifferent parents are to be treated no differently from the involved and the peripheral. All materials should be shared and an effort made to help such parents to confront the claim of Christ. Realistically, however, we know that not all such efforts will bear fruit. In such a case, some form of sponsors should be selected from among adults in the church, and such persons should be assigned to a young person. They should be people who like young persons and who will take their responsibility with real seriousness. Such a relationship should not cease with baptism but continue, so that the young person has a sense of a "family" within the church.

MARKS OF ADOLESCENCE

Adolescence is a new phenomenon. Earlier societies had no such period. The adult world was entered directly from childhood. With the development of industrialized society, the age at which youth entered the adult world was later than formerly. The reason for this is clear; greater skills were required, and so the period of training and education had to be prolonged. Adolescence is that extended period.

There is no denying the fact that many find this period a difficult one with which to deal. Parents, teachers, and society generally join in a chorus of concern and perplexity. It is no accident that the adolescent years are so often referred to as times of "storm and stress." I am not arguing that such reactions are not understandable, but I do contend that we can deal helpfully with adolescents only when we make a real effort to understand, if only in a rudimentary fashion, some of the dynamics operating in young people during these years. A search for a real understanding will lead to the writings of people like Erik Erikson and Edgar Friedenberg. Only a quick outline of some of the areas of growth and development is offered here.

Sexual development. The adolescent years encompass the pubertal development. There is a significant change in the attitude of the adolescent toward the self and toward others. Sometimes this growth poses problems in understanding, and the dynamic sexual change creates real problems of adjustment. In addition, the late years of adolescence bring sexual maturity; indeed, the sexual drive is then at its strongest. This area of sexual development needs to be put within the context of a wholesome total outlook, a task in which religion must play an important role.

Movement toward independence. The child is marked by almost total dependence upon the home and parental decision making. The adolescent moves away from such dependence toward some real independence. The power to make important decisions is moved during the years of adolescence from the parents to the young person. This transferal is always a somewhat difficult task, because what seems to the parents wise and gradual will often seem to the adolescent silly and slow. Tensions are inevitable in this area, but it needs to be recognized that the goal of all concerned should be the emergence of autonomous moral personalities.

Achievement of greater emotional maturity. The child has little ability to control responses; what is felt is expressed. The adolescent is in the difficult period of learning how to substitute some creative responses for destructive ones, and this task is often very demanding because the young person has neither the full maturity of the adult nor the free impulsiveness of the child. A certain awkwardness is natural in such circumstances.

Movement toward economic independence. It is in the years of adolescence that the young person arrives at an assessment of his or her abilities and makes the pivotally important choice of a vocation.

With the lengthening of the years of schooling beyond the actual adolescent period, there is not so much actual entrance into the world of work. Nevertheless, that day is definitely approached, and adolescence is usually the time when vocational possibilities are seriously examined and a choice is often made.

Formation of a religious outlook. The adolescent is very much concerned about determining who he or she is and to what a commitment can be made. Authority is questioned during these years, and it is no longer sufficient to issue edicts and expect the adolescent to accept them with no questioning. The larger issues of the nature of the universe and the person's place in it emerge in a serious fashion during adolescence. Thus, there is an openness to possibilities during these years, and a Christian faith presented with real power can elicit a deep commitment on the part of adolescents

AIMS OF DISCIPLESHIP TRAINING

These adolescents, then, are the young persons who will be involved in discipleship training. Not only do we need to understand them well, but we also need to have clarity about our aims. Vital discipleship training should include the following goals:

1. The presentation of the claim of Jesus Christ in as effective manner as possible. I repeat what I said earlier about the danger of manipulation, but I also affirm that our goal is to bring young persons to the place where they can honestly decide for themselves about the Christian faith. This means a knowledge of what the Christian faith actually is, a familiarity with its basic document, the Bible, and with the life of the Christian community.

2. The incorporation of young persons into the life of the believing community through believers' baptism. The church is a central and basic part of the Christian life, and it is only through the sharing of its life that the Christian finds power and direction for effective service. While the church needs always to be kept under judgment, it is the Body of Christ and our task is to bring persons into its life.

3. Participation with God in his mission in the world. It is not enough to enlist persons in the church. God has a mission to be carried on in the common life, and the church is effective in the service of God and neighbor when its members are dispersed to bear witness in the world of everyday existence.

CHAPTER 5

Discipleship Training for Young People

The leader of a discipleship training venture has a tremendous opportunity and a frightening responsibility. Such a person must enter into the world of the adolescent with sympathy and understanding. Utilizing the insights gained from psychology and experience, the leader seeks that point where the world of adolescence encounters Jesus Christ. If that encounter does not take place, in whatever ways are appropriate, discipleship training has failed in its basic purpose.

We make certain assumptions. The leader of such a group needs to be a committed person, aware of what faith is all about and able to communicate effectively the bearing of faith on daily life. Furthermore, the leader needs not only to understand young people but also genuinely to like them. A final assumption is that all preparations have been carefully made. Contacts have been established with the homes of the young people. Some sort of covenant has been established in regard to regular attendance and participation. All materials are in hand and physical arrangements, which are of considerable importance, are in readiness.

I want to share in this chapter two actual discipleship training ventures. One will be three separate class sessions. The second will be a weekend retreat. These ventures have the merit of actually having been used to good effect; there is nothing theoretical about them.

THE CLASS SESSIONS[1]

Since it is young people who are to be involved in these sessions, certain techniques will be helpful. One is to provide variety in the types of presentation. The material should not all be presented by lecture. There should be many chances for discussion. Action and

[1]Materials in this section have been developed by David W. Swink.

33

movement are important for young people, and the sessions make it possible to have some movement.

In general terms, the class sessions, held from 1:30–3:30 on Saturday afternoons, were structured in this way (see Appendix A for the materials used):

Class Session #1

Goals:

> To learn each person's name and something about him/her.
>
> To ascertain the maturity and knowledge level of each person.
>
> To review and expand biblical knowledge and biblical use.
>
> To help each person begin to understand the nature of the church and the two Baptist ordinances.

Anticipated Participation: twelve to fifteen people and two leaders.

Procedural Breakdown:

1. General overview and "Getting to know you" session—1:30–1:45
2. Diagnostic test—1:45–2:15
3. Bible knowledge and usage—2:15–2:50
   Introduction, nature of the Bible, and its development; "Who, What, When, and Where?" game (adapted from TV quiz show)
4. The nature of the church and its history—2:50–3:20
   The two Baptist ordinances
   Tour of the church building
   > Basement—church history
   > Gym—church community and play
   > Baptistry and baptismal dressing area—meaning and nature of baptism (historical and current)
   > Chancel area—Lord's Supper
   > Balcony—worship
5. Fellowship time—Youth lounge with pop and cookies—3:20–3:30
6. Homework assignment—Bring to the next class session something, a book, an article, a tape recording, which has had an important influence on your life. Be ready to share it.

Class Session #2

Goals:

> To begin to learn more about ourselves as far as what influences and motivates us.

To come to some understanding of the nature and definition of sin.

To learn the important aspects of Jesus' life and teachings.

Procedural Breakdown:
1. Sharing together—1:30–1:45
   a. What was learned that was new
      (1.) Game to increase Bible knowledge—"Quick Draw"
      (2.) Discussion about Jesus
      (3.) Return tests from last week
   b. What motivates us
      (1.) What each person brought in
      (2.) What each person thought
2. The nature of our humanity and of sin—1:45–2:30
   a. Short lecture on who we are and instructions for the drama
   b. Drama—use episodes in the Bible to portray the nature of sin
3. The life and teachings of Jesus—2:30–3:20
   a. Short introduction
   b. Music game, using Handel's *Messiah, Godspell,* and *Jesus Christ Superstar*
   c. Effects—time line of church history
4. Fellowship in Youth Lounge—3:20–3:30

Class Session #3

Goals:

To understand better the meaning of discipleship in order to make intelligent decisions.

To gain an initial knowledge of church history, especially in relationship to the Baptist denomination.

To continue to use the Bible so that we can more readily identify its different sections and understand its correct meaning.

To gain a deeper insight into the concepts of Christian theology.

Procedural Breakdown:
1. Sharing together—1:30–1:45
   a. Look over and discuss extra work.
   b. Have slides available which show church history.
   c. Use "Who, What, When and Where" Bible knowledge game.
2. Sharing of stories of the twelve apostles—1:45–2:05
3. Church history—using time line and discussion—2:05–2:20
4. Snack break—2:20–2:30

5. Looking at and discussing Statement of Faith—2:30–2:45
6. Test and discussion—2:45–3:20
7. Details on Sunday's meeting with the board of deacons—3:20–3:30

MEMBERSHIP CLASS RETREAT[2]

The class sessions will be the form used in most of the churches. But this procedure is not the only choice available, and there is often wisdom in varying the methods used from year to year. If there is a feeling that a new way of proceeding is needed, the membership class retreat is a possibility. It provides a setting and an opportunity for intensive consideration of what discipleship means. It has the additional advantage of providing a chance for those considering discipleship to meet in a common experience with those who have already made a commitment, giving those who have made a commitment a chance to recognize that such commitment is a process, not an event only, and to reflect upon what their subsequent experience has meant to them.

Certain preparations have to be made. When this option was used, a tentative outline of the retreat was drawn up by the ministers and shared with the board of deacons. A meeting followed with the teachers of the junior high classes in the church school, in which their cooperation was enlisted. An initial letter was sent to all parents informing them of the plans and asking for their cooperation in the venture. Further revisions of the plans then took place, with a second letter being sent to all parents. On a given Sunday, a registration form was distributed to the young people.

What follows is a capsule description of the actual retreat. Eighteen junior highs and four adults went on the retreat.

Saturday morning

9:30—Leave the church for camp.

11:00—Arrive and get settled.

11:15—First Session

"Who Am I?" Stick-on name tags were made with the names of famous people (movie and TV stars, celebrities, athletes). A name tag was put on the back of each young person. Each person was then asked to show the group his/her "name," and an individual in the group had to pantomime the famous person until the young person guessed who he/she was.

[2]Materials in this section have been developed by Robert G. Middleton, Jr.

This activity was chosen because the young people would be so keyed up about being on the retreat, plus having spent an hour and a half in a car, that it would be impossible to get into a serious discussion right away. But it furnished a chance to say to the junior highs that they were there for something more than just to roam around the camp. It also provided an opportunity for some of the youth to demonstrate abilities unknown until that time and furnished a chance for adults to enter into the experience as one of the group.

(An evaluation of this particular part of the retreat was favorable, but with as many as twenty-two persons sharing, there is a danger that it may take too long.)

Saturday afternoon

12:30—Lunch

1:00—Free time given to allow the group to get a breath of fresh air and to work off some excess energy.

1:30—**Second Session**

"What Does It Mean to Be a Christian?" This question formed the focus for the second session. The minister spoke for fifteen or twenty minutes, dealing with various accounts of persons who had responded to Jesus' challenge to "Come, follow me" (Matthew 4:18-22; Luke 19:1-10; Acts 9:1-9). In addition to figures from the New Testament, some modern followers were also selected, so that the young people would have a sense that commitment to Jesus is a vital, live option in the present. Following the talk, the question was raised, "What does it mean to you to be a follower of Jesus?" Magazines, newsprint, scissors, and glue were provided, and each person was asked to respond to this question by making a collage. After each individual had made one, the group was called back together, and each person talked about his or her collage.

A session such as this can be very productive and positive. The tone will be set by the opening discussion of what it means to respond to the invitation of Jesus. This is no step to be taken lightly, and the talk should stress this fact. The making of the collages gave the junior highs something to *do,* which at their age is important. It also helped them to realize that they can communicate through means other than verbal exchanges. Pictures often say things better than words.

3:30-5:30—Free time—basketball, snowball fights, hikes.

5:30—Dinner. Meal provided by the camp.

Saturday evening

7:00—**Third Session**

"What Does It Mean to Belong to a Community of Faith?" The group was shown the film *Baptism: Sacrament of Belonging.* This film was made by the Franciscans and is part of their TeleKETICS series. Although made by Roman Catholics, it is very appropriate for Protestant use. The film runs about ten minutes. Following the showing of the film, the group was divided into two sections—one was composed of those who were considering baptism; the other, those who had been baptized. Members of each group reacted to the film from their own particular perspective. Beginning with the film, the discussion moved to the meaning of baptism in their lives.

(This discussion was, for the leader, the highlight of the retreat. Deep feelings were expressed by the youth in terms of what had happened to them as they faced their decision in regard to Christian discipleship or, if they had already made the decision, what it had meant to them.) After the two groups had had a chance to discuss the film separately, they came back together to view the film in the light of their discussions.

9:00—Recreation

11:00—Everyone in the building

12:00—Lights out!

1:30—Quiet—at last!

Sunday morning

8:00—Breakfast

9:00—**Fourth session**

"The Church as a Particular Community of Faith." The session began with a review of what had been done on Saturday, trying to highlight some of the discussions and activities which had been significant. Then the group read together the account of the baptism of Jesus by John (Matthew 3:13-17). The total group then divided into the two groups mentioned previously—those who had become members of the church and those who were contemplating this commitment. One group looked at the account of the early church in Acts and identified some of the activities carried on by the church and asked what the modern church ought to be doing. Those who had made their commitment reflected on what they had found in the church.

11:15—Worship

The worship was designed to be an outgrowth of what had been happening. The Beatitudes were read (Matthew 5:1-12). A prayer was recited which had been prepared by members of the group. A song was played from an album by Ken Medema called "Fork in the Road." Following this, each person was asked to go off alone and reflect on what he or she had been thinking about during the time together and what decision had been made. Then the group came back together for a closing prayer.

12:00—Lunch and back to the church.

ONE-TO-ONE

There will, of course, be times when there will not be a number of young persons thinking of church membership. However, even one young person has a claim on the church's best training. The materials to be covered are the same as for class sessions: the Christian faith in God; the nature of God; the mission of Jesus Christ; the human predicament (sin and its consequences); the meaning of redemption; the significance of the church; the meaning of baptism and the Lord's Supper; and the history of the people called Baptists. Because there is only one person, the teaching can move faster than with a group.

The class sessions, the retreat, and one-to-one training are methods which can be used. If nothing of this sort is being done, serious thought needs to be given to the responsibility of the church and ministers to guide persons in Christian growth. If something is now being done, there is perhaps room for improvement and for the use of new techniques. What is essential is that we recognize that Christian growth begins with careful training.

CHAPTER 6

Preparing Adults
for
Church Membership

The Christian task is not only the conversion of the world. It is the conversion of the church as well. The church itself is constantly in need of renewal; this is not a condition encountered at rare intervals. What we confront today is a situation in which the church is not only the *agent* of mission; it is also the *field* of mission.

In light of this situation, the church can take nothing for granted. Because the mission we confront is of such tremendous importance, the training we provide for all must be the best we can possibly devise. This applies to those we have already considered in previous chapters—children growing up, young people making their commitment. What we advocate in this final chapter is a corresponding need to provide training for adults as well.

To do this well requires a recognition that training and growth are indispensable parts of our Christian life, and a significant responsibility of the church is to provide a context within which such growth and training can take place. The Christian life, viewed in this perspective, is a pilgrimage; the Christian is always on the way, and a major peril to the enterprise is the assumption that one has arrived. Such arrival is really impossible in the light of the summons: "You, therefore, must be perfect, as your heavenly Father is perfect" (Matthew 5:48).

ADULT CANDIDATES FOR MEMBERSHIP

There are basically three groups of adults seeking membership in most of our churches. (1) There are those who have never previously made a Christian commitment. (2) There are others who are transferring membership from another denomination. (3) There are those who are moving membership from one Baptist congregation to another. While there are differences among these three groups, there is enough similarity to permit the same basic training material to be shared with all. If they have made a previous commitment, a review of what a Christian believes will be helpful; and Baptists, as well as those who come from other denominational backgrounds, can always stand a review of what Baptists believe.

The material, then, can be shared with all three groups, with some minor modifications. What will have to be determined is the scope of the training to be offered and the regulations governing admission to church membership.

Tensions arise when we attempt to determine two matters: the scope of training and the vexing question whether such training is to be voluntary or mandatory. It is obvious that no one can determine either question for Baptist congregations, but one can suggest that the issue needs to be faced head-on. It may be helpful if we mention briefly some of the possibilities and the tensions.

Some feel that admission to the church should be no more difficult than it was in the New Testament. The earliest confession was a simple one: ". . . Jesus is Lord . . ." (Romans 10:9). The directness of the New Testament witness is revealed also in Acts 16:31: "Believe in the Lord Jesus, and you will be saved, you and your household." Here, it is said, confession of faith is the essential matter, and there is no denying such a contention. Nothing can be done without that confession of faith. There is unanimity, I believe, on the proposition that such an affirmation is the *beginning*; the question comes as to whether that is also the conclusion. The contention in these pages is that a period of training following the initial confession of faith is vitally important.

Those who are uncomfortable about requirements may wish to make training sessions voluntary on the part of those who are accepted into the membership of the church. New members may be encouraged to attend; they will not be compelled to do so. This is one possible way by which to avoid what seem to be external requirements.

The alternative is to decide that some training is an essential part of the Christian discipline and to require that all persons seeking membership undergo a period of training. Where this is required, it is sometimes in advance of admission and sometimes following admission. It is, however, clearly expected that all persons, no matter by what means they are coming to the church, will participate in the training sessions.

There are certainly good arguments to be made on both sides of this issue. No resolution of the matter is attempted here, but a suggestion is offered. Whatever is finally decided, let it be on the basis of something more significant than expediency. When the issue is confronted in a congregation, the crucial question to be asked is: what is required of us as people of God if we are to fulfill our calling? That's the question which ought to be confronted, and all too often that is the last question asked.

In addition to the question of whether training is to be voluntary or mandatory, there is the question of duration of the training. Once again there is a wide variety of practice and possibility. Some churches (a minority, I am sure) require a lengthy period, sometimes stretching over a couple of years. More common is the practice of a training period covering a number of weeks, usually from three to six or eight sessions.

Since Baptist congregations will undoubtedly vary in their practice, I want to share a number of possible outlines. Perhaps there will be value in trying different ways of doing the training, following some of the suggestions offered here and then adapting such suggestions, until you arrive at a way of proceeding which best fits your own need.

EXTENDED TRAINING

The Church of the Saviour in Washington, D.C., has long been an exciting venture. Begun originally out of disenchantment with typical church life, it has remained a small and dynamic Christian fellowship. There has not been great growth, and the congregation has had to face up to the problem this creates in a culture which is oriented toward "success." That issue has been faced and the members have forthrightly determined that the smallness of the group will be accepted and that they will be concerned only about the essential meaning of being a congregation of Christ's people.

The story of the venture has been written by Elizabeth O'Connor. Her book *Call to Commitment* tells the story in a splendid manner and helps us to understand how this group of Christians could merit the praise of Elton Trueblood:

> The Church of the Saviour is the most encouraging Christian fellowship known to me. It is encouraging because it takes seriously the notion that the Church is meant to be a redemptive fellowship rather than a religious equivalent of secular promotion.[1]

If we seek to understand how this small group could come to merit

[1]Elizabeth O'Connor, *Call to Commitment* (New York: Harper & Row, Publishers, 1963), p. ix.

such praise, we shall find it in the realism of the demands and in the care taken with training.

The demands are very real. Here is the minimum discipline for members:

We covenant with Christ and one another to:

Meet God daily in a set time of prayer

Let God confront us daily through the Scriptures

Grow in love for the brotherhood and all people, remembering the command, "Love one another as I have loved you."

Worship weekly—normally with our church

Be a vital contributing member of one of the groups

Give proportionately, beginning at a tithe of our incomes

Confess and ask the help of our fellowship should we fail in these expressions of devotion.[2]

A couple of things should be noted about this minimum discipline. The first is that one can become a member and so live under this discipline only after the completion of two years of a prescribed course of study, which will be outlined below. The second thing to note is that in October of *each year* members are asked to recommit themselves. This discipline states: "Each year, under God, we will review our commitment to this expression of the Church. If we find at any time this doesn't have meaning for us or we are automatically performing a ritual, we will not recommit."[3] Great care is taken to prevent the discipline from becoming a lifeless kind of legalism.

It is against such a background that we should look at the course of study carried on in the Church of the Saviour.[4] There are five areas covered: (1) Old and New Testaments, (2) Christian Growth, (3) Christian Doctrine, (4) Christian Ethics, and (5) Stewardship. Let us look in summary fashion at the highlights covered in each of these areas.

(1) Old and New Testaments

Old Testament

Giving of the Covenant to Moses and the Israelites

The development of the Hebrew nation

The message of the prophets

The prophecy of the Messiah

New Testament

The fulfillment of the prophecy in Jesus

The life of Jesus

[2]*Ibid.*, p. 34.
[3]*Ibid.*, p. 36.
[4]*Ibid.*, see pp. 193-200 for a full description of these courses.

The giving of the New Covenant
The development of the Gospels
The growth of the Twelve
The call of Paul
The growth of the church

(2) Christian Growth
The practice of daily prayer
The place of the Scriptures in the Christian life
The place of corporate worship in the Christian life

(3) Christian Doctrine
Creation and the understanding of the Bible
The "Fall"—the meaning of sin and evil
Beginning the Great Redemption and the meaning of God's revelation of himself
A chosen people and the meaning of election
The need of a mediator or redeemer and understanding of our finiteness
Christ—the high point of history
Christ's death and resurrection
The Holy Spirit, grace, and the birth of the church
The doctrine of last things, heaven and hell, and the meaning of mission

(4) Christian Ethics
Nature of God as revealed in Jesus Christ
Nature of humanity in relation to the demands of God
The dilemma of the moral person in an immoral society
Choosing between a lesser and a greater evil
Personal ethical issues
  Truth-telling
  Stewardship of time
  Recreation
  Group loyalties
  Courtship and marriage
  Search for a creative vocation
Social issues
  State and politics
  Labor and economic issues
  War and peace
  (Note: This course is often taught by giving careful attention to a study of the Sermon on the Mount [Matthew, chapters 5–7] and the application of its teachings to daily life.)

(5) Stewardship

  Assignment: the writing of a page on one's philosophy of the use of time and a tabulation of the way in which time is actually spent.

  Assignment: the filling out of a report of one's financial status and a discussion of this with another member of the group.

  Assignment: the relating of a personal incident of sacrificial giving, akin to that of Mary in breaking the alabaster box of ointment.

  Assignment: the writing of a paper on one's darkest and loneliest moment.

  (Note: The members of this course are all committed persons who seek a deep level of Christian devotion.)

ALTERNATIVE SESSIONS

I have provided this sort of outline of what is being done in one creative Christian congregation, not because I think that it can or should be duplicated in ordinary church fellowships, but because I think it serves as a kind of corrective to our lack of concern about training. It would not be possible to institute such a program in many of our churches, for a variety of reasons. But this program does suggest that there are Christian groups who take with real seriousness the matter of training.

If such a program is too ambitious, many congregations can utilize with great profit some of the procedures now in use in Baptist churches. Eleanor Menke summarized such courses in the *Baptist Leader*.[5] Here are some procedures in actual use which she outlines:

Walter Pulliam, of the First Baptist Church of Seattle, Washington, outlines a four-week session. All persons who seek to join the church, whether by letter or experience, are expected to attend the four sessions. Attendance, which must be prior to the baptism, is required for all who seek baptism. The sessions are held on Sunday mornings at the church school hour.

First Sunday. The focus in this session is on the local church, in this case the First Baptist Church of Seattle. The history, mission, and organization of the church are shared with the prospective members. The bylaws are reviewed, usually by a lay person. In addition, there is a sharing of current emphases and ministries.

Second Sunday. The second session turns to the basic matters of Christian belief. The concept of God is explored and special emphasis

[5]Eleanor Menke, "Preparation for Responsible Adult Church Membership," *Baptist Leader,* January, 1974, pp. 63-64.

is given to the growing understanding of God in the Old Testament.

Third Sunday. The life, ministry, and mission of Jesus Christ form the core of the third session. Included in this is the growth of the church as the unfolding of the meaning of Christ's work.

Fourth Sunday. The story of the church through the centuries forms the basis of this session. In this session the history of Baptists receives special attention, together with the emphases which have been a special part of Baptist life and witness. Note is also taken in this session of the ecumenical age and the ways in which Baptists work with other Christian bodies.

A somewhat more flexible and open type of approach is shared by Richard P. Olson, of the First Baptist Church of Racine, Wisconsin. The sessions are not called "Church Membership Classes," but "Inquirer's Group." In keeping with the idea of flexibility, the group does not always meet at the same time. It may meet in the morning or evening or daytime; the time depends upon the schedules and desires of those interested. The group is not composed solely of those seeking membership. As the name implies, it is open to any who have questions about the meaning of Christian faith or who, though already members, wish to gain deeper insight into the meaning of such membership.

The content for the sessions consists of two parts. One part comes from the questions raised by members of the group, and the second is a statement by the pastor which deals with basic Christian convictions, the privileges and responsibilities of church membership, and the Baptist heritage.

A time of decision is provided at the end of each group series. At this time, the pastor discusses with the members, either individually or in a group, whether they wish to make a decision or whether they feel they need further time and study. The decision properly is left with the person.

John Bartos, of the First Baptist Church of Haverhill, Massachusetts, has developed a course of study which covers five or six weeks. The heart of the program is a concern for individual commitment to Jesus Christ as Lord and Savior. It is recognized that such commitment issues in responsible participation in the life of the church and that the church must have at the heart of its life a concern for the Great Commission.

The basic matters considered in the sessions are:

1. *The Introduction.* Here it is emphasized that our beliefs determine our way of living. Always we are accountable to God for

our actions, and the Bible is presented as the indispensable guide for us in daily living.

2. *God's Plan of Salvation for All Mankind.* The meaning of sin and our need of redemption are considered here.

3. *The Ordinances.* The meaning of the ordinances of baptism and the Lord's Supper is explored, setting forth the origin of the rites in Christ's teaching.

4. *The Church of Jesus Christ.* Christians live under the mandate of the Great Commission. This session explores the way in which the American Baptist Churches in the U.S.A. seek to fulfill that commission. The role of the believer in sharing responsibly in this mission is considered also.

5. *Christians and the Life Hereafter.* The biblical concepts of heaven and hell are explored, and emphasis is placed upon the significance of Jesus Christ as the way to eternal life.

6. *Our Church Covenant.* The covenant is studied and evaluated. It is emphasized that the covenant is a guide, more than a set of rules.

Conclusion

This manual has sought to do two things: (1) to share a concern about the relative ineffectiveness of our Christian witness today, and (2) to suggest some ways by which this condition may be remedied. A final word must be to stress that the renewal of our churches will not happen by the development of better techniques alone; it is not, finally, a matter of programs, because such programs are dependent upon a motivation which they cannot supply themselves. The only way to the renewal of the churches is for increased devotion to be exemplified in local churches throughout our land. If it doesn't happen in our local churches, as we often say, it won't happen at all. Better training for Christian discipleship will not solve all our problems of Christian witness, but it is surely an indispensable starting point.

Materials for Discipleship Training Class Sessions

DIAGNOSTIC TEST—DISCIPLESHIP CLASS

Check the answer that is the best answer for each question.

1. You are coming to the discipleship class because:
   a. You have nothing to do on Saturday afternoon.
   b. Your parents threatened you if you did not come.
   c. Your best friend was coming and asked you to come along.
   d. You want to learn more about the Christian faith and life-style.

2. The (name of church) is:
   a. A building on the corner of (list street).
   b. A library with books about God and missionaries.
   c. A group of Christians who worship together in the Baptist tradition.
   d. A zoo with all the animals God made.

3. Jesus of Nazareth is a man who:
   a. Lived long ago in a country called Israel.
   b. Lived a good life and was called "rabbi."
   c. Lived, was put to death, and rose again from the dead so that we might know God's love for us.
   d. I don't know who he is.

4. The disciples of Jesus were:
   a. Rich and important men.
   b. Fishermen who gave up fishing to become followers.
   c. Crazy people who went about the country doing nothing and living off welfare.
   d. Roman spies.

5. To become a disciple of Jesus you must:

   a. Score 100 on this test.

   b. Memorize all of the New Testament.

   c. Be willing to base your life on God's love and try to live your life by following Jesus' example.

   d. Join the church so you can take Communion with your friends.

6. The Bible is:

   a. Divided into two sections—the Old and New Testaments.

   b. A result of many writers who were led by God and who wrote over a long period of time.

   c. The guide book for Christians.

   d. None of the above.

   e. All of the above.

7. When we worship God, we are:

   a. Sleeping because we stayed up to watch the late movie on Saturday night.

   b. Joining together with other people who believe as we do in order to praise God and ask for his help.

   c. Afraid the adults sitting behind us will catch us passing notes.

   d. Helping the person next to us.

8. Baptism is:

   a. What you have to do to be a church member.

   b. Following Jesus' example.

   c. A symbol of our entering into a new covenant with God.

9. The Lord's Supper is:

   a. A symbol of Jesus' death and resurrection by which we know God's love.

   b, The way we can tell if someone is a church member or not.

   c. None of the above.

10. The pastor of the church is:

    a. The spiritual leader of a group of people.

    b. The person in a black robe who leads in the worship service.

    c. A poor basketball player.

    d. Somebody I am afraid of.

MATCHING

Write the correct name in front of the phrase that describes that title.

1. Paul   _____The city that ruled the world.

2. Moses   _____The first man, according to the Hebrew creation story.

3. Peter   _____The place where followers of Jesus were first called Christians.

4. Isaiah   _____The prophet who wrote of the Suffering Servant.

5. Amos   _____The Holy City of David.

6. Adam   _____Led the children of Israel out of Egypt.

7. Judas   _____The first Christian missionary to the Gentiles.

8. Rome   _____Betrayed Jesus of Nazareth.

9. Jerusalem_____Was called the "Rock."

10. Antioch   _____A letter written by Paul.

11. Romans _____The prophet who called for justice especially for poor people.

TRUE OR FALSE

Write the word "true" or "false" on the blank preceding each of the following statements.

1. _____A fish was the symbol of the early Christian church.

2. _____Jesus taught that we should love God and our friends.

3. _____A good Indian is a dead Indian.

4. _____Living a Christian life means giving up everything.

5. _____Prayer is talking with God.

6. _____My parents are good people.

7. _____Jesus taught by telling stories.

8. _____The Christian church is very old.

9. _____Martin Luther was a leader of black people who was killed in 1968.

10. _____The Christian faith has nothing to do with the rest of life.

DISCUSSION

Everyone *must* answer the first question. Then choose between questions two and three, and answer just *one* of those two questions.

1. Since you are here today, I assume you are considering becoming a follower of Jesus Christ and joining the church. Please tell me in your own words what becoming a Christian means to you. Do you think it will make a difference in your life? If so, how?

2. Write an account of Jesus of Nazareth's life as if you were a reporter for the Detroit *Free Press* and this was to be the cover story for the Sunday edition. Include in your story all the important facts, as well as saying what you think of his life, death, and resurrection.

3. The Christian church began after Jesus' resurrection and has continued since then. What is the church? What is its history? And, what does it mean to you today?

SUMMARY TEST FOR THE DISCIPLESHIP CLASS

Biblical Knowledge: Please answer the following questions in complete sentences.

1. What are the two divisions in the Bible?

2. What are the names of the four Gospels? What do these books tell us about?

3. Name two of the books of the Prophets.

4. Name two letters of Paul.

5. What is the book in the Old Testament which tells us about the Hebrew understanding of the creation of the world?

6. Where can we find Jesus' Sermon on the Mount?

7. How can the Bible help us in our lives today?

8. What was the original language of the New Testament?

Historical Knowledge: Check each statement that is *TRUE* for the given name or place.

1. Moses:
   ____Led the people of Israel out of Egypt.
   ____Was put in a reed basket as a baby.
   ____Built the temple of Jerusalem.
   ____Received the Ten Commandments on Mt. Sinai.

2. Paul:
   ____Was named Saul and persecuted the Christians.
   ____Was one of the twelve disciples of Christ.
   ____Wrote the letters to the churches included in the Bible.
   ____Was the first Christian missionary to the Gentiles.

3. Peter:
   ____Tax collector whom Jesus called to be a disciple.
   ____Denied Jesus three times before the cock crowed.
   ____Was called the "Rock" because Jesus saw in him the qualities of a leader.
   ____Leader of the apostles who said Jesus was the Son of God.

4. Isaiah:
   ____Prophet who wrote of the Suffering Servant.
   ____Prophet who was swallowed by a big fish.
   ____Man chosen by God to build an ark.
   ____Became king and played a harp.

5. Amos:
   ____Prophet who was a favorite son and wore a coat of many colors.
   ____Prophet who called for justice especially for poor people.
   ____Believed God was holy and believed worship should be holy.
   ____Was paralyzed but was healed by Abraham.

6. Adam:
   ——Broke his relationship with God and others.
   ——Was the first man, according to the Hebrew creation story.
   ——Was a man whose name means "ground."
   ——Lived in the Garden of Gethsemane.

7. Judas:
   ——Disciple who was sorry for what he did and hung himself.
   ——Disciple of Jesus who betrayed him to Jewish authorities.
   ——Came from Kerioth near the town of Hebron in Judah.
   ——Made a bargain for thirty pieces of silver.

8. Antioch:
   ——The place where Moses received the Ten Commandments.
   ——The place where Paul began his mission journeys.
   ——The place where followers of Jesus were first called Christians.
   ——The city that Isaiah prophesied would be destroyed.

9. Romans:
   ——The people of Rome.
   ——People who conquered the world.
   ——A letter written by Paul.
   ——The people who ruled the world in the time Jesus lived.

10. Jerusalem:
   ——City where Jesus was born.
   ——City where Jesus was killed.
   ——City which was destroyed in A.D. 70.
   ——The Holy City of David.

11. Martin Luther:
   ——Leader of the Protestant Reformation.
   ——Leader of black people who was killed in 1968.
   ——Nailed the 95 theses to a door to challenge the pope.
   ——Taught that Jesus came to free us from the law.

12. The Baptist church:
   ——Was first begun in England around 1600.
   ——Was established after breaking off from the Congregationalist church.
   ——Believes that all people can enter into relationship with God.
   ——Believes that adult baptism by immersion is the correct way of baptism.

Theological Knowledge: Complete each sentence.

1. Deciding to become a disciple of Jesus Christ means

2. The church of Jesus Christ is

3. God is

4. Jesus Christ is

5. Being baptized will mean

6. By participating in the Lord's Supper, I

7. When I worship, I

8. Prayer is

9. Sin means

10. The minister of a church is

CHALLENGE SECTION

1. Prepare a collage on what "church" means to you today.

2. Answer the Bible knowledge quiz.

3. Uncramble the "Word Scramble."

4. Work the crossword puzzle.

5. Read a book from the book list. (See page 62.)

6. Identify the people in the "Who Am I?" list.

BIBLE QUIZ

1. Which bird was considered ceremonially clean for use in the temple worship?

2. The Bible tells of an earthquake, "And the earth did shake and the rocks were rent." When did this happen?

3. The town where Jesus lived as a boy was _____.

4. How many books are there in the New Testament?

5. How many of these are letters written by apostles?

6. What was the name of a man who collected taxes on behalf of the Romans?

7. Which book of the Bible is a collection of poetry and hymns?

8. Which books of the Bible are called Wisdom Books?

9. Which one of the gifts brought by the Wise Men was a sweet smelling gum found on shrubs in the desert?

10. Which books of the Bible are called the Pentateuch?

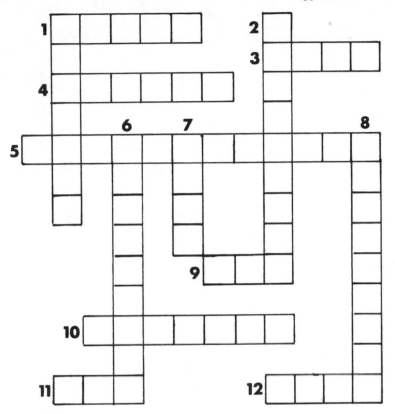

ACROSS:

1. Books of sacred writings in which God reveals himself.
3. Another word for sacred.
4. Speaking to God.
5. The act of learning and following a master.
9. A broken relationship with God.
10. A person who tells what he sees or experiences.
11. Given responsibility to care for God's earth.
12. Prophet who preached truth, honesty, and righteousness.

DOWN:

1. A Christian symbol signifying rebirth.
2. A person who believes in Jesus Christ.
6. Sharing a part of yourself with someone else.
7. The first Christian missionary to the Gentiles.
8. Men dedicated to keep every Jewish law in every detail.

WHO AM I?

1. **AAMD**   A man who was brought up as an Egyptian.

2. **BASAABRB** A seamstress who was raised from the dead by Peter.

3. **SEMOS**   The man named for ground.

4. **HOJAN**   A released bandit.

5. **SRUCOD**   A prophet who refused to follow God's direction.

WORD SCRAMBLE

1. **LTIAPE**   ☐☐☐☐☐☐   The ruler who washed his hands of Jesus' death.

2. **BBRASUAN**   ☐☐☐☐☐☐☐   Paul's companion on the first trip.

3. **VADDI**   ☐☐☐☐☐   A shepherd boy who became king of Israel.

4. **HWAHEY**   ☐☐☐☐☐☐   Hebrew word for God.

5. **OHAN**   ☐☐☐☐   The man who built the ark.

6. **TURH**   ☐☐☐☐   The wife of Boaz.

7. **HERTSE**   ☐☐☐☐☐☐   A Jewish wife who saved her people from death.

8. **INELDA**   ☐☐☐☐☐☐   He prayed three times daily even when the king told him not to do so.

9. **STHHEABBA**   ☐☐☐☐☐☐☐☐☐   The mother of Solomon.

◯◯◯◯ ◯◯◯◯◯◯   One of the persons of the Trinity.

TIME LINE OF CHURCH HISTORY

Abraham trusts God's call and moves to Palestine

King David builds Jerusalem into the capital city

Jesus is born in Bethlehem

All of the books of the New Testament are written by

The great cathedrals of Europe are constructed

The English Baptist congregation is first begun

3000 1280 1000 587 B.C.—0—A.D. 50 100 300 1100 1500 1600 1870

The Exodus of the Hebrew people out of Egypt

Jerusalem is destroyed

Paul establishes new churches

St. Augustine unites Greek and Hebrew thought

Martin Luther begins the Reformation

The First Baptist Church of Birmingham is begun

Resources for Discipleship Training

NEW MANUALS:

Joseph and Arline Ban, *The New Disciple*—for Juniors and Junior Highs

Loren D. McBain and L. Doward McBain, *Born Again and Living Up to It*—for Senior Highs and Adults

FOR CHILDREN'S DISCIPLESHIP TRAINING

General

BOOKS

Lulu Hathaway, *Partners in Teaching Older Children.* Valley Forge: Judson Press, 1971.

Linda Isham, *On Behalf of Children.* Valley Forge: Judson Press, 1975.

Ronald Goldman, *Readiness for Religion.* New York: The Seabury Press, Inc., 1970.

Lois Horton Young, *Dimensions for Happening.* Valley Forge: Judson Press, 1971.

Hymns and Songs of the Spirit. Valley Forge: Judson Press, 1966.

Hymnal for Juniors in Worship and Study. Philadelphia: The Westminster Press, 1966.

Norman H. Maring and Winthrop S. Hudson, *A Short Baptist Manual of Polity and Practice.* Valley Forge: Judson Press, 1965.

Using the Bible (Resources to be used with third and/or fourth graders)

BOOKS

Paul B. and Mary Carolyn Maves, *Learning More About Your Bible.* Nashville: Abingdon Press, 1973.

The Young Reader's Bible. Philadelphia: A. J. Holman Company, 1966. Distributed by Abingdon Press.

Samuel Terrien, *Golden Bible Atlas.* New York: Golden Press, imprint of Western Publishing Co., Inc., 1957.

AUDIOVISUALS

Stories About Jesus. Color filmstrip.
The Bible Through the Centuries. Color filmstrip.

The Baptist Story

BOOKS

Ed Clayton, *Martin Luther King: The Peaceful Warrior.* 3rd. ed. Englewood Cliffs, N.J.: Prentice-Hall, Inc., 1968.

Benjamin P. Browne, *Tales of Baptist Daring.* Valley Forge: Judson Press, 1961.

AUDIOVISUALS

Bright Are the Promises. Color filmstrip.

BACKGROUND MATERIALS FOR USE WITH YOUTH AND ADULTS

BOOKS

Dietrich Bonhoeffer, *The Cost of Discipleship.* New York: The Macmillan Co., 1967. Paperback.

David H. Read, *The Christian Faith.* Nashville: Abingdon Press, 1969.

John S. Whale, *Christian Doctrine.* New York: Cambridge University Press, 1941.

Culbert G. Rutenber, *The Reconciling Gospel.* Valley Forge: Judson Press, 1960.

Culbert G. Rutenber, *The Price and the Prize.* Valley Forge: Judson Press, 1953.

Harvey Cox, *God's Revolution and Man's Responsibility.* Valley Forge: Judson Press, 1965.

Norman H. Maring and Winthrop S. Hudson, *A Baptist Manual of Polity and Practice.* Valley Forge: Judson Press, 1963.

Robert G. Torbet, *The Baptist Story.* Valley Forge: Judson Press, 1957.

AUDIOVISUALS

These may be selected from the catalog of American Baptist Films, available from American Baptist Films, Valley Forge, PA 19481 or American Baptist Films, Box 23204, Oakland, CA 94623. The filmstrip *This Is My Heritage* is especially appropriate.